How D
There is a God?
The Bible is True?

Reasons Young People Can Believe

Lynn Waller

ISBN 9781704090160

Published by Send Love with Books

sendlovewithbooks.com

Dedication

To my grandsons, Casen and Keaton Kilmer, whom I am confident will grow up to be strong men of God

Acknowledgements

Special thanks to:

Dr. Kelly Felps (Internal Medicine) for his help on the chapter "Clues from the human body" and

Dr. Hugh Henderson (Physicist) for his many valuable suggestions, especially dealing with scientific matters.

About the Author

Lynn Waller has also written *The International Children's Bible Dictionary* (Word Publishing, 1987, 1997), *How Do We Know the Bible Is True* (Zondervan, 1991) and contributed to five other books. In addition he has written several articles for journals dealing with biblical, historical, and educational subjects and spoken to teacher groups on those topics. In 2009 he spoke at the Christian Scholars Conference at Lipscomb University. He earned a B.A. in Biblical Studies, an M.A. in Church History from Abilene Christian University and has done additional postgraduate study in history and education from the University of Texas at Arlington and the University of North Texas.

He and his wife, Jan, have two adult children, Landon Waller and Wendy Kilmer (married to Scott), of whom they are very proud.

Table of Contents

How Do We Know There Is a God?

How Do We Know the Bible Is True?

Section 1

How Do We Know
There is a God?

Part 1 Clues from Man

Where did right and wrong come from?

One hot summer night I was coaching a softball game and the batter on the opposing team hit a ball that went straight down, bouncing off home plate and rolled to the pitcher. The pitcher threw to first, putting the batter out. But the umpire yelled, "Foul ball." I ran out of the dugout, "Why?" The umpire replied, "Home plate is in foul territory."

I said, "No, home plate is in fair territory!" After a little arguing, I finally said, "Look in your rulebook and see whether home plate is foul or fair." Unfortunately nobody at the game had a rulebook. The next day the umpire checked the rules and discovered that home plate is fair.

That umpire and I had an argument about whether the batter was out or not because we had different ideas about what is a foul and fair ball. But we agreed that there are certain rules that govern how the game is played. We were just arguing about who understood the rules better.

All over the world at all times in history people have said that there are certain rules that everyone ought to live by. Let's say person A slaps person B. What will B say? "You shouldn't hit me like that!" or "Why did you do that?" Then A will usually defend himself by saying it was an accident, self-defense, B deserved it for being rude or some similar explanation.

There is something quite important to notice in this discussion between A and B. Though they may argue over who did something wrong, without realizing it, both are agreeing that you shouldn't hurt people unless you have a real good reason. Some people have different ideas about what is good enough. But everyone believes in the general rule, "Don't hurt people."

In different times and places throughout the world there are and have been some differences in ideas about right and wrong. But deep down almost everyone has had the same basic sense of how we should treat each other. C. S. Lewis described it this way in his book **Mere Christianity**:

> Think of a country where people were admired for running away in battle, or a man felt proud of double crossing all the people who had been kindest to him. You might just as well imagine a country where two and two made five.[1]

Every now and then you may find a person who says he doesn't believe in the real Right and Wrong. But if you treat him wrong, he will say, "That's not fair." Which shows that he really does believe in that Right and Wrong; he just sometimes doesn't want to keep it.

The more you think about it, the clearer it should be that all people on this earth have had this basic sense of Right and Wrong. But where did this come from? The best explanation is that it came from the same place man did. Christians say that God is responsible for us being here. Not only that, but he is trying to bring us closer to himself. Our sense of Right and Wrong is one clue that there is Someone who is trying to steer us toward the Right.

Part 2 Clues from Nature

Is the Woodpecker Just Hardheaded?

A friend of mine once told me about being in a biology class when a student asked the teacher this question, "How can a woodpecker beat his head against a tree hard enough to drill holes in without shaking his brains to pieces?"

The teacher answered, "Don't worry about the woodpecker. He can take care of himself." It's a shame that teacher didn't know more about woodpeckers, because the student asked a very good question.

Woodpeckers have so many unusual features. For example their feet are not like other birds. They have two toes pointing forward and two pointing backward. That enables them to hook onto a tree trunk instead of perching on a branch. Their tail feathers are shorter and stiffer than other birds. This also helps them hook on to the side of a tree.

Other birds have a beak and a skull that are fused together, but the woodpecker has a pad of spongy tissue between them that acts as a shock absorber. The woodpecker drills holes to find insects that eat into wood. But after finding the insects' tunnels, he can't get to the insects unless he has a much longer tongue than other birds. Guess what? He does. The tongue is normally attached to the back of the mouth. But that isn't long enough to do the woodpecker any good. Instead his tongue circles around inside his skull and is attached to the top of his head. A woodpecker needs a tongue as long as his body. Built this way, he can have one.

The woodpecker needs each of the special features: shock absorber, special toes, short stubby tail and a long tongue. He could not survive without all of them. Someone gave the woodpecker exactly what he needed.

European Green Woodpecker's tongue

The Language of the Bees

Bees may be small but they have probably been studied more than any other creature besides man. Scientists have discovered some fascinating information about them.

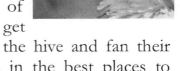

To start with, the developing larva must be kept at the right temperature. The bees have a remarkable way of cooling them if the weather starts to get too warm. First they bring water to the hive and fan their wings. They even station themselves in the best places to achieve the most efficient airflow.

Perhaps the most amazing thing is how a bee who finds food communicates it to the rest of the hive. The bee who has found something returns to the honeycomb and dances across it. If he goes straight up the comb, it means that food can be found by flying straight toward the sun. Dancing down the comb means fly away from the sun. By varying the angle of their movements, they can tell the exact direction.

In addition, how long and how loudly the scout bee dances tells the others how faraway the food is. This allows the bees to know how much honey to take with them so as to have enough energy to make it. And they take only enough to get them there. That way they will have room in their body to bring extra food back to the hive.

The honeycomb is made in hexagon shaped cells. Scientists have discovered that this exact shape gives the greatest volume and strength with the least material. Who taught the bees how to communicate so precisely and how do they know the perfect shape for their honeycomb? It makes you wonder.

What's So Great about Water

Water is something we see and drink every day. In fact no living thing can live without it. Even a huge number of chemical reactions will not occur unless water is present to help the process. In many ways life and chemistry depend on water. So it is fortunate that this all-important liquid has some extraordinary characteristics.

Water is the only substance that is a liquid at temperatures suitable for life and also forms a vapor that is lighter than air. If this alone were not true, life as we know it could not exist.

Another interesting fact about water is that it is able to dissolve so many solid chemicals. A large number of solid chemicals needed to keep plants and animals alive must be dissolved in a liquid. For plants it's sap and for animals it's blood (both of which are made of water). No other liquid can dissolve even half

13

the necessary solids. (The only exceptions are some acids, but they would dissolve our bodies as well.) Water is perfect. It dissolves everything we need it to, but not our body organs.

Water is also unusual in the way that it holds heat better than almost anything else. This helps make our weather more bearable. It also helps all mammals maintain their body temperatures even when the air temperature goes up and down.

Also water has the strange characteristic of expanding as it gets colder. Almost everything else gets smaller as it cools. It seems normal to us for ice to float. If it were like most things, it would sink. But it doesn't and that is helpful because when water freezes, it breaks up rocks. This causes the soil to be enriched.

Similarly, water freezes from the top, not the bottom. If it were the other way around, animals living in the water could not survive. This is because they would lose much of their food supply and protection from enemies. Our climate and many other natural forces would be changed for the worse if it were not for that one fact that water starts freezing from the top.

For us to live we not only need water, but we need it to act in certain ways. And in every single case, it acts just like we need it to. Isn't that lucky for us? Or is it luck?

Living Dangerously

Several small creatures have remarkable ways of surviving. One of the most interesting is the bombardier beetle. This creature defends himself with a sort of flame thrower. It is almost like the fire breathing dragon in fairy tales. But this bombardier beetle is quite real. He does it by mixing two dangerous chemicals with two enzymes that cause the

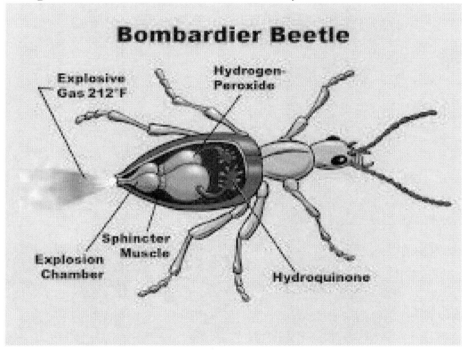

Bombardier Beetle

Explosive Gas 212°F

Hydrogen Peroxide

Sphincter Muscle

Explosion Chamber

Hydroquinone

explosion.

The explosive chemicals are made in separate glands and stored in different organs. The combustion chamber for the mixture is at the back of the beetle's body. This chamber is lined with a protective covering and has an opening he can aim at the enemy. When an enemy is near, the bombardier beetle mixes his four chemicals in the explosion chamber. Then bam! The predator is sprayed with a blast of fire.

Every tiny part of this complicated system has to work perfectly or the beetle would lose his defense or burn himself up.

Another example of this dangerous precision is the North American conifer sawfly. The larva of this insect eats mainly

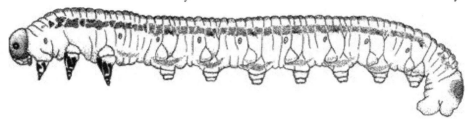

pine needles. The needles are full of a sticky substance that is poisonous to insects. But the sawfly eats the digestible part of the needle and separates the poison into sacs in its head. Instead of getting rid of this poison, the sawfly saves it until he is attacked and sprays it on his enemy. Quite a feat!

Some sea slugs perform a similar trick. These slugs like to eat creatures with whip-like stingers. They somehow keep their prey from using their stingers and then swallow them. Now here's

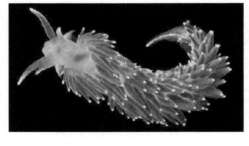

the weird part. The sea slug's stomach has passageways leading from the stomach out to his back. His stomach digests everything except the harmful stingers. They slide out these passageways to his back. Then he uses the stingers on his enemy.

Did these amazing, precise arrangements come about by

accident? It looks more like someone carefully designed these on purpose.

How Has Man Survived?

Have you ever wondered how people survived from dangerous creatures before the days of modern technology? For example, in Africa man would be no match for a lion. But fortunately, lions do not like human flesh. Occasionally there is a man eating lion, but they are rare and an oddity. In fact, in Africa the only large meat eaters who like humans are hyenas and crocodiles. The crocodiles are easy to avoid. Stay out of the water where they are. Hyenas are too afraid of people to attack unless the person is wounded or asleep.

In other areas of the world the situation is about the same. The only large creatures that like human flesh are in the water where we don't live. If lions, wolves and bears liked to eat humans, we would have been extinct long ago. But the creatures that could have wiped us out, prefer other meat.

Many insects and spiders can be deadly to man, but they usually attack only in self-defense. Most people know about the South American piranha. A group of these fish can turn a swimming man into a skeleton in a few minutes. We are very lucky that piranhas are fish, not rats. If rats had the same jaws and appetites as piranhas, man would have had major problems.

How has all this happened? Scientific researcher Dr. Alan Hayward answers:

It does indeed look as if man owes his survival to a mind. But not his own puny mind. It seems much more likely that man is here because the Mind behind the nature has kept all our potential executioners in check.[1]

Where Are You Going, Eels?

Eels are a really unusual fish. They are so long (3 to 6 feet) that they look like a snake. When eels are young they are so thin and transparent you could read the words on this page through their bodies.

The most interesting thing about eels concerns their migration. American and European eels live in freshwater streams on different continents until they are 5 to 15 years old. Then they swim down to the Atlantic Ocean stopping in waters near Bermuda called the Sargasso Sea. There the adults spawn (lay eggs) and die. When the young ones are just a few inches long, they suddenly start on an unbelievable journey.

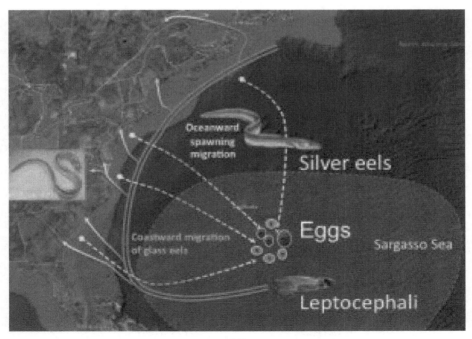

They head back to the freshwater streams of Europe and America where their parents had lived.

It takes those American eels more than a year to swim through the ocean and up the river where they finish growing up.

The European eels have longer to go and it takes them three years. Remember these baby eels make this amazing trip without the help of their parents who died back in the Sargasso Sea.

This is truly one of nature's most astounding stories. It is so amazing that Noel prize-winning biologist George Wald said that this behavior of the eels looks as if a mind is at work and "this conclusion embarrasses biologists".[2] However, this doesn't embarrass all biologists. Those who believe in God are not embarrassed at all.

Nature's Best Dressed Birds

Someone has said, "All you have to do is look at an ostrich, a giraffe or a penguin to know that God has a sense of humor." That may be true, but studying such animals can also show us some marvelous examples of God's design.

There are several kinds of penguins. The large emperor penguin has very interesting nesting habits. At the beginning of autumn the female leaves the ocean and lays one large egg on the bare ice. The male then holds the egg on his feet, which are covered by folds of skin to keep it warm. He must stand around for about two months waiting for the egg to hatch.

Meanwhile the female has gone back to the ocean to feed. She returns just in time for the egg to hatch. She is able to pick out her mate and chick from the often hundreds of thousands of other penguins. She feeds the chick partly digested fish she has caught at sea. If the female were only a day or two late the little one would die. But that mother knows exactly when to arrive!

Now the father does the same thing. He's out in the ocean for two weeks. He arrives just in time for the next feeding, bringing fish stored in his body.

As Lawrence Richards says in his book *It Couldn't Just Happen:*

> Patterns like this which occur again and again in the animal world, are evidence of careful planning and design . . . how easy to see the hand of God.[3]

Part 3 Clues from the Human Body

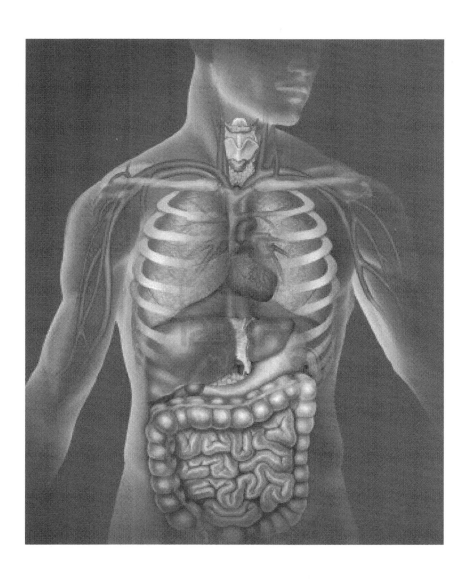

The World's Most Amazing Camera

The first cameras were invented in the early part of the 1800's. They were large, heavy and hard to use. The person being photographed had to sit very still or the picture would blur. Of course everything came out in black and white. But in the last 150 years as men have  learned more of the science involved in photography, cameras have gotten much better. Not only are pictures now in color, we can photograph people who are running full speed.

But long before man invented these, we already had in our body the most amazing camera, the human eye. Whoever designed our eyes did some remarkable work. If our eyeball were any other shape we could see only straight ahead. But because it is round and has a group of muscles attached to it, it can move left, right, up and down. He has also provided a liquid (tears) to wash and lubricate the eye, as well as sponges (eyelids) to wipe it. There is even a pipe to carry the extra liquid away to the nose to drain (which is why we have to blow our nose if we cry a lot).

This amazing eye is protected in several ways. First of all, it is located in exactly the right place. If the eye were sticking out of our forehead, it wouldn't last long. It would be too easy to get hit and ruined. But the eyes are set back into our head so that they are protected by the skull and the nose.

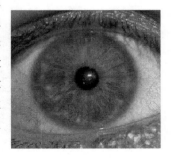

To work properly our eyes need a covering that is clear, strong and flexible. And that is exactly what the cornea is.

As men have experimented with light, optics and everything involved in photography, cameras have been developed that can adjust to bright light. For the last 150 years bright minds have worked to make great improvements in the camera. The more successful they are, the closer they come to the remarkable camera that has been built into all of us all along. Whoever designed that camera must have known a great deal about light, optics and many other scientific principles. "Does he who formed the eye not see?" (Psalm 94: 9b)

The Pipeline

Imagine a tube running under the ocean that comes to the surface at every inhabited island. It also crosses every continent and branches out to reach every city, every street and even passes right beside every person on earth. Now imagine that this open tube has running water in it. Floating on the water are little rafts with every kind of food in the world: fruit, vegetables, meat, cereals, and desserts. The tube flows past all 4 billion people on earth. Each person has only to reach down and pick out whatever he wants. Somewhere along the pipeline new items are put in to replace each one taken out.

This sounds like a neat idea, but too impossible to ever happen. But wait! It already exists, inside our body. You've probably guessed that it's our circulatory system. Our blood vessels flow not just to 4 billion, but 100 trillion cells in our body. Each cell takes what it needs and puts in wastes that are not needed.

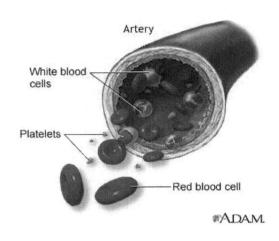

As you probably know, these nutrients are carried in the red blood cells. But there are also two other kinds of blood cells floating in this marvelous fluid called blood. White blood cells rush to any part of the body where they are needed to fight infection. The third kind of blood cells are platelets. They help the blood form a clot or scab to keep us from losing too much blood if we have a cut.

As we mentioned, the blood not only carries nutrients to each cell, it also carries away harmful wastes from the cells. The blood is constantly being filtered through the kidneys to remove these wastes. If something goes wrong with a person's kidneys, there is a dialysis machine. The sick person's blood can be run through a dialysis machine regularly to do what the kidneys normally do. This machine is about the size of a suitcase. But our natural one (the kidney) weighs only one pound.

If anyone could build the pipeline we described, it would be the greatest engineering achievement of all time. But someone did design one in miniature inside each one of us. [1]

Three Doctors Look at the Body

Recently I asked a friend of mine, Dr. Kelly Felps, (specialist in internal medicine) this question, "In your study of the human body what have you found that convinces you that God is real?"

I found his answers interesting. The first fact he mentioned is the amazing way the body heals itself. Cuts and broken bones grow back together. Germs and infections or fought off by the body's own defenses. Many tissues that are lost are automatically replaced. What doctors really do is just help the body heal itself. As Dr. Felps said, "God is investing energy in our system. All true healing comes from God."

The second fact concerns the mysteries of the mind. The body has been studied more than any other area of science. Yet we have only scratched the surface of understanding ourselves. We know that certain areas of the brain are responsible for seeing, hearing, tasting, etc. But where do thoughts and ideas come from? What about man's creativity, imagination, and his thoughts about doing good to others. These traits separate us from the animals. These are good evidences that we really are created in God's image.

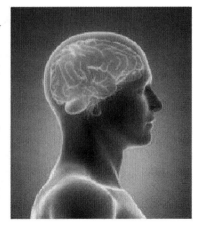

Dr. Don England (a chemist) in his book *God, Are You Really There?* also talks about the brain. It only weighs 3 pounds but contains 900 billion neuralgia. These are special supporting and connecting cells. This huge number of cells along with the other parts of the brain will fit in the space smaller than a shoebox. From that little area man can think, reason, create, love, decide and worship.

Every day computers become more a part of our lives. They can store and make available great amounts of information. Computers are designed by sharp minds. In fact computer researchers study how the brain works to improve the design of their computers. But who designed the brain? Dr. England answers, "The human brain, by its design, is an architectural masterpiece which only Deity [God] could contrive [think of]." [2]

The story of Dr. Francis Collins, one of the world's leading scientists, can teach us a lot. Collins did not believe in God as a student in medical school. But he noticed something about patients who were in great pain, but had a strong faith in God. Their trust in God gave them a peace even when suffering. He found that amazing.

It made him start rethinking his rejection of God. He realized that the idea of a real Right and Wrong (see the first chapter of this book) made good sense. Reading *Mere Christianity* by C.S. Lewis helped him come to a full faith in God and become a Christian.

It was as a believer that he made scientific news with his discovery of how DNA works in making up all the parts of a person's body. Collins said that with this knowledge, we are "learning the language in which God created life."

He is convinced that this scientific knowledge should make us feel awe that God has given us such a wonderful gift. Dr. Collins added that it was truly exciting "to realize that we have caught the first glimpse of our own instruction book, previously known only to God."[3]

Part 4 Clues from the Universe

The Lucky Planet

Human beings can't live just anywhere. For us to live there are many conditions that have to be just right. Here are some of the ways that planet Earth is exactly right.

(1) The Right Kind of Sun

Some stars (Suns) give off too much heat; others not enough. Some flare up every now and then, which would destroy any life depending on them. Our sun gives out just the right amount of steady light and heat. In the *Star Wars* movies advanced civilizations live in "a galaxy far, far, away". But astrophysicist Hugh Ross points out in his book *The Improbable Planet* that as astronomers can see farther into the galaxies, they have not found one even close to being suitable for advanced life.[1]

(2) The Right Distance

Of the eight (or nine) planets in our solar system, only Earth is the proper distance from the sun to sustain life. Venus and Mars are the closest planets to us. But the temperature on Venus gets up to 500° C. (Way too hot!) On Mars our first space probe recorded a temperature of 86° below zero. (Way too cold!)

(3) The Right Size

If the planet is too small, it doesn't have enough gravity to hold liquids and gases on its surface. Large planets have too much gravity and would make it too hard for living things to move around.

(4) The Right Kind of Rotation

Our planet rotates once every 24 hours. Most of the other planets do it much more slowly. Venus, for example, takes 243 of our days to turn once. Rotating so slowly makes it far too hot during the day and much too cold at night.

(5) The Right Materials

Living things are made up mostly of water, carbon, oxygen, hydrogen and nitrogen. The universe seems to be short of all these except hydrogen. But guess where you can find plenty of the other five of these? That's right, our lucky planet.

(6) The Right Amount of Ocean

About 4/5 of the Earth's surface is covered with water. If there were much less ocean, the land would be desert. If there were a lot more ocean, the remaining land would get so much rain, life would be difficult at best.

(7) The Right Kind of Atmosphere

The air we breathe has about 78% nitrogen, 21% oxygen, and only .003% carbon dioxide. These proportions are balanced just right to keep both plants and animals alive. Similarly, if our air was as thick as Venus or as thin as Mars, we could not live.

These are just a few examples. There are many more.[2] Are we just incredibly lucky, or did Someone plan all this? I know which one makes more sense.

What Holds It All Together?

What is it that keeps us all on the earth and not floating off into space? Of course it's gravitation. But there's more to it than that. Gravitation means that every object in the universe has an attraction for every other object. The attraction is greater the larger and closer together the objects are. The smaller or farther away, the less the attraction. This simple principle of attraction is actually necessary for our universe to work.

Notice how it's involved in space travel. In the late 1960s and early 1970s the Apollo space program sent several manned spacecraft to the moon and back. It took great rocket thrust for the spacecraft to overcome the huge attraction of the Earth's gravitation. However, as the rocket moved farther from the earth, the less pull the Earth's gravity had.

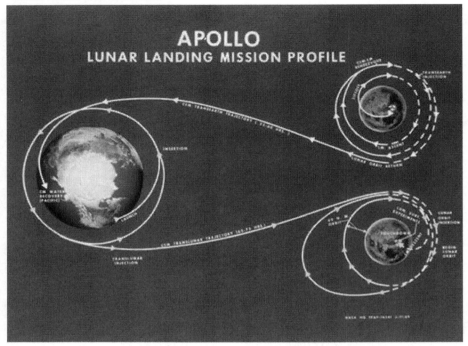

At some point on the way to the moon, the moon had more attraction on the rocket than the Earth. This helped pull the spacecraft faster toward the moon. When it was time to blast off from the moon, it was easier than leaving the Earth. This is because the smaller moon has less gravitational attraction than the earth did on the first blastoff.

As the Apollo moved away from the moon, the attraction lessened. The closer it got to Earth, the faster the rocket moved because the Earth's pull was growing. So actually, the whole round-trip was made possible by this universal attraction or gravitation. In fact all the stars and planets keep their positions due to the law of gravitation. It seems that gravity is holding the universe together. But is there an even greater force behind gravity? Yes there is! It is Christ, the son of God. Not only was he involved in the creation, but the

Bible tells us that "in him all things hold together." (Colossians 1:17)

What Scientists Have Discovered

"Mathematics is the alphabet with which God has written the universe."

This was said by Galileo (1564-1642) who is called the founder of modern experimental science. He improved the telescope and discovered the first four moons of Jupiter and many other facts of astronomy. Modern science was begun by people who believed that God had designed order in the universe. So if man experimented and observed carefully, he could discover these principles of the universe. As these scientists learned more about the world, it confirmed their faith in the God who is behind it.

Isaac Newton (1642-1727) is considered one of the greatest thinkers in history due to his discoveries in mathematics, physics and astronomy. He is probably most famous for being the first to express the laws of gravitation. Newton saw God at work throughout nature. He said, "In the absence of any other proof, my thumb alone would convince me of God's existence."

In 1687 he published his first book, ***Principles of Mathematics***. In it he wrote:

> The most beautiful system of the sun, planets and comets could only proceed from the counsel and dominion [mind and power] of an intelligent and powerful being.[3]

Isaac Newton had learned from Johannes Kepler (1571-1630) who discovered the three laws of how the planets move. Kepler, a German mathematician and astronomer, said:

> Since we astronomers are priests of the highest God in regard to the book of nature, it befits us to be thoughtful not to the glory of our minds, but rather, above all else, of the glory of God.[4]

Many more examples could be given from other founders of various areas of scientific investigation. But we might look at the more recent story of Dr. Boris Dotsenko, head of the Nuclear Laboratory in Kiev, Russia. For many years he believed there was no God. But he was interested in studying the law of entropy. This is a scientific principle which says that in time everything tends to decay, fall apart or become disorganized. The more Dr. Dotsenko thought about it, he realized that there must be a great power that keeps the universe organized, or else the whole world would have turned to dust long ago. He wrote:

> There must be a God-one God-controlling everything! I realize that even the most brilliant scientists in the best equipped laboratories are still incapable of copying even the simplest living cell. God must be the creator of life on earth.[5]

Several astronauts have reported being especially impressed with the reality of God while out in space. For example, Jack Lousma was the pilot of Skylab 3 in 1973 and a member of the Apollo-Soyuz mission in 1975. His experiences led him to say:

I now have a much greater appreciation for the world that God has created. It's clear in my mind that this would not have happened by chance.[6]

More Recent Discoveries

Some scientists who don't believe in God have argued that the universe has always been here. But recent discoveries have made that harder to believe. One of the most exciting was the measurements made by the COBE (Cosmic Background Explorer) satellite in 1990 and 1992. It gave dramatic evidence that the universe began with an awesome explosion. When interviewed on ABC television's Nightline, one scientist commented that this new information helps show the truth of Genesis 1:3 "And God said, 'Let there be light, and there was light'".

Astrophysicist Dr. Hugh Ross reports that this new information from the COBE satellite as well as other recent discoveries has had a great impact on the scientific world. Many scientists who doubted that there was a God are now changing their mind. One of them was Paul Davies who wrote:

> [There] is for me powerful evidence that there is something going on behind it all . . . it seems as though somebody has fine tuned nature's numbers to make the universe. . . The impression of design is overwhelming.[7]

Astronomer George Greenstein said it this way:

> Is it possible that suddenly, without intending to, we have stumbled upon scientific proof of the existence of God? Was it God who stepped down and so providentially crafted the cosmos for our benefit?[8]

Dr. Ross is often asked why so much new evidence for God has come to light lately. In other words why have we been given more proof than people in earlier times? His answer is that the resistance to God in our time is high. So many are trying to reject God, that he allows more evidence to come to light.

What Does It Mean?

In light of all this, two important facts need to be remembered. First of all, the universe is expanding. The galaxies are rapidly moving away from each other. Now it's clear that this couldn't have always been happening. If we go far enough back, they must've been once been very close together and started moving outward. But what started the movement? Something or Someone started everything.

The second fact is that the universe is running down. Isaac Newton noticed that (unless new energy is added) warm things always cool off and cold ones get warmer. So he concluded that the universe must have been created with a supply of energy that is being used up. This principle is now called the Second Law of Thermodynamics.

Here's an example. Our Sun is made up mostly of hydrogen. It's light and heat come from burning that hydrogen. In a few million years it will run out of hydrogen. The universe is like a ship in the middle of the ocean. The fuel tanks are now half full. If you found such a ship steaming across the ocean, you would know that someone originally filled those tanks and started it going. But who originally filled the universe's fuel tanks with hydrogen and set up the conditions for that fuel to be turned into heat at the proper rate? There are still many scientists who answer the question the same way Newton did: the Creator[10]

Suppose you were riding in your car that was leading you across the border from the United States to Canada. As you cross into Canada, you see on a hillside large white stones neatly spelling out, "Welcome to Canada."

You remark to a friend riding with you, "Isn't that nice of someone to greet us that way. I wonder who went to all that trouble to spell that out on the hillside."

But your friend answers, "No one did. Rocks are always falling down hills. Those rocks just happened to land that way."

You would think, "What's wrong with this guy?" The message on the hillside is a clear indication of someone's design and plan. Our universe is saying the same thing.

> "The heavens tell the glory of God, And the skies announce what his hands have made." (Psalm 19:1

Part 5 Faith in God Changes People and the World

Results of Believing in God

What would we think of people who would take little babies and put them out in the cold to suffer and die. We would say that it's terrible and ought to be stopped! Well, 2000 years ago that was common practice. For example, people might want a boy, but a girl was born. So, they would just throw away the baby girl.

Guess who stopped that awful practice? Was that atheists or Christians? Of course, it was the followers of Jesus. He was the one who said, "Let the little children come to me, and do not hinder them." (Matthew 19:14 NIV)

In our country every week we see thousands of people gather in huge stadiums to watch sports events. This also

37

happened in the Roman Coliseum at the time of Christ. But they came to watch people fight against lions and other wild beasts. There were also matches between gladiators. These were well armed men who fought each other until one was killed.

It was Christians who finally stopped this bloody and cruel business. These early followers of Jesus showed the world how people ought to treat one another. Historian Adolf Harnack reported that early Christians set a good example in several other areas:

(1) They gave money generously to help widows, orphans and other poor people. (2) They started hospitals to care for the sick. (3) much care and concern was shown to prisoners and people working in unhealthy mines. (4) Slaves were treated as human beings and often their freedom was purchased by church funds. (5) In times of epidemics and disasters they organized to relieve the suffering around them. (6) Christians paid for the burial of those who were too poor to have a decent burial. (7) They tried to find jobs for people who needed them and gave food to those who are out of work.[1]

Christians have not always done as well as we should have in these areas. But it's important to remember that most of the efforts to make this world a better place has come from those who "were longing for a better country-a heavenly country." (Hebrews 11:16)

Changed Lives

In the 1800s a well-known atheist named Charles Bradlaugh challenged Hugh Price Hughes to debate the truth of the Christian faith. Hughes was a minister who worked with poor people in London. He agreed to debate on one condition.

Hughes suggested that one way to help prove who was right would be for each to bring a number of people whose lives were turned around by that teaching. Hughes said, "I'll bring 100 people whose lives were a mess until they turned to God. You bring 100 people whose lives were a mess until they turned away from God." Later Hughes told Bradlaugh that if he couldn't find a 100, then 50 would do. Then he lowered it to 20 and finally to one. Hughes would bring 100 people whose lives were changed by God while Bradlaugh would only have to find one person whose life was changed to better by becoming an unbeliever. Bradlaugh couldn't do it.

That's not surprising. People aren't improved by turning to atheism. People are improved by turning to God. There are so many thrilling stories of this truth in action. You may not have heard of Mary Slessor. She was from Scotland, but in 1876 she went to an area of Africa called Calabar. The people who lived there were so wild and savage, no one went near there. Their behavior was awful. They thought twins were bad luck, so they killed them as soon as they were born. Then they took the mother out and let her be eaten by wild animals. They also had many slaves and regularly ate them.

It was here that Mary Slessor went to take the story of the love of God. She started by rescuing twins. The people of that area thought twins were bad luck and often let them die. She personally rescued hundreds of twins, caring for them as long as needed and adopted five of them as her own children.

When wars between tribes were about to break out, she would run out and stand between them to prevent the fighting.

She taught the adults about the Son of God who died for them. And they listened. In village after village people started turning their lives over to God. When they did that, their savage, cruel behavior stopped.

One could tell of the Auca Indians in Ecuador in more recent times. In the 1950s they killed any outsider who entered their land. The first missionaries (Jim Elliot and four others) who came there did not come out alive. But the next group were able to tell about the love of God, and that Auca tribe turned to Christ. Not only did they quit their killing, many even became missionaries spreading the Good News of Jesus to other tribes. One of those who killed Jim Elliott would later count on his fingers and say, "I have killed twelve people with my spear! But I did that when my heart was black. Now Jesus' blood has washed my heart clean, so I don't live like that anymore."

History is full of dramatic stories of people, famous and unknown, rich and poor, young and old, whose troubled lives have been changed by their faith in God.

Part 6 The Bible Reveals the True God

What Else Should We Know?

Throughout this book we have tried to look at the world around us watching for clues that God is behind it all. Those clues can be found in the way people act, how animals live, the way the universe works, and what happens when people find the true God. But there's one more place we need to look. There is a book filled with information about God. Of course that's the Bible.

The Bible has been around for a long time. Many people have examined the Scriptures to see if it's reliable. Over and over again it has proven its accuracy. So, if our knowledge of God is going to be complete, we must look there.

The Bible tells us to look around us and see God at work. Remember what Psalm 19 said,

> The heavens tell the glory of God. And the skies announce what his hands have made. Day after day they tell the story. Night after night they tell it again. (Psalm 19:1-2)

There is one whole chapter on this subject that is most interesting, Psalm 104. There the Scripture shows the orderly way God makes nature work.

> You make the grass grow for cattle, And vegetables for the people- You make food grow from the earth. (Psalm 104:14)

The passage goes on to show how trees provide homes for birds. Also notice in verse 18:

> The high mountains belong to the wild goats; Rocks are hiding places for the badgers.

People in ancient times often thought mountains and rocky places had no value, since they couldn't farm or raise livestock there. The Bible says those places may not be worth much to man, but God made them just right for badgers and wild goats. We might look at Antarctica and think that's a useless place, frozen all year round. But the penguins think it's great. It's just right for them.

Now look at verses 24-25:

> Lord, you have made many things. With your wisdom you made them all. The earth is full of your riches. Look at the sea, so big and wide. Its creatures large and small cannot be counted.

So, we should see God's wisdom in the many creatures he has put on this earth. Notice that it says the sea is huge and full of living things. Most of those millions of sea creatures are never seen by man. Another Psalm says, "Praise the Lord from the earth, you large sea animals and all the oceans." (Psalm 148:7) I like what John Piper wrote about this:

> Why did God create great sea monsters? Just to play, to frolic in the ocean where no man can see, but only God? The teeming ocean declares the glory of God, and praises him 1000 miles from any human eye. [1]

So many places in the Scripture tell us we ought to see God in the universe around us. But there's more to it than that. Look at Psalm 8:3-4.

> I look at the heavens, which you made with your fingers. I see the moon and stars, which you created. But why are people even important to you? Why do you take care of human beings?

Looking at the awesomeness of all that God has made should cause us to look at ourselves and be amazed (and happy) that God cares for us as small as we may be.

Don't Stop Yet

We have looked at many good reasons for believing in God. But just knowing that there is a God is not enough. We need to know who God is. There are many different ideas of God. Some are pretty close to being correct, others are way off base. When the apostle Paul spoke to the educated people of Athens, he started by noticing that they had many statues of gods in their city. But the true God was unknown to them. So he told him some things they needed to know about God:

> The God who made the world and everything in it is the Lord of heaven and earth and does not live in temples built by hands. (Acts 17:24) (NIV)

All through history people have limited God to certain times and places. Paul says God is too great for that. As you read Paul's speech, he is emphasizing that we must know the real God and know what he is really like. Believing in just any God will not work.

Secondly, just knowing about the true God is not enough. We must have a relationship with him. As Paul said, "God wanted them to look for him and perhaps search all around for him and find him. But he is not far from any of us." (Acts 17:27)

The New Testament letter called *Hebrews* adds this:

> Without faith no one can please God. Anyone who comes to God must believe that he is real and that he rewards those who truly want to find him. (Hebrews 11:6)

We must not just believe that God is there. We must also believe that he is the kind of God who rewards people who really want to know him. Christians believe in the God who created the whole universe and loves all people even though we have done wrong and don't deserve it. He proved it by sending his son, Jesus, to die for us. Let us keep on searching the Scriptures to know God and his love better.

Section 2

How Do We Know

the Bible Is True?

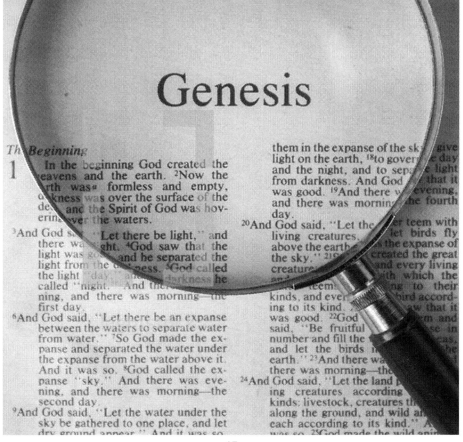

Science in the Bible

In our modern world, almost everyone knows that it's important to keep clean. But people haven't always known that. In fact, it was less than two hundred years ago that we discovered it.

In the 1840s, a doctor in Austria named Ignaz Semmelweis was concerned about the women in his hospital. Too many of the mothers who were there to have a baby were dying. He wanted to find out why.

Dr. Semmelweis noticed that many of the women were being treated by doctors who had just finished doing autopsies. (An autopsy is an operation on a dead person to find out why he died.) After the autopsies, the doctors would examine the live patients without washing their hands first. So Dr. Semmelweis decided to try a new rule: All doctors and nurses had to wash their hands after handling the dead bodies before they could touch the live patients.

Guess what happened? The number of deaths went down immediately.

Later, Dr. Semmelweis tried his discovery at another hospital. It worked beautifully there too.

Within the next thirty years, scientific discoveries about germs proved that Dr. Semmelweis was right, and why. But really, Dr. Semmelweis wasn't the first to know that cleanliness is healthy. It had been in the Bible for more than 3,000 years!

God told Moses in the book of Numbers, chapter 19, to wash after touching a dead body. Also, in Leviticus 13 and 14, God told the Israelites how to keep open sores and other skin diseases from spreading.

It took man thousands of years to find out why those things were in the Bible.

What holds up the earth? That question has puzzled mankind for thousands of years. In India, they thought the earth was resting on the backs of several large elephants. The elephants were resting on the back of a very large turtle. The turtle was either resting on a snake or swimming in a sea of milk.

Others said the earth was on the back of a catfish swimming in an ocean. According to the Greeks, a god named Atlas had the difficult job of holding the earth on his shoulders.

But the Bible says that God "hangs the earth on nothing" (Job 26:7). And today we know that that is true: The earth is suspended in space. It isn't sitting on anything!

But when the book of Job was written, people didn't know that. How did the writers of the Bible know it? Only God could have revealed it to them.

Another thing people believed in biblical times (and for hundreds of years afterward) was that the earth was flat. If you went too far, you would fall off the edge!

Now, of course, we know that the earth is round. In

the 1500s Ferdinand Magellan's men were the first to sail all the way around the world. That helped prove the roundness of the earth.

But that too was revealed in Scripture long before man discovered it. For example, Isaiah 40:22 says, "God sits on his throne above the circle of the earth."

The roundness of the earth is shown in another way in Luke 17. There Jesus tells about his Second Coming. He said, "On that night two people will be in one bed; one will be taken and the other left. Two women will be grinding grain together; one will be taken and the other left" (NIV). So when Christ comes again, it will be night for some people but the next verse tells us it will be daytime for others..

How can it he daylight and dark at the same time? If the earth is flat, it can 't. But the earth is round, and that means it's always daytime on one side and night on the other. They didn't know that in Jesus' time. But he did. And there it is in the Bible.

The earth as seen from the moon by the Apollo 11 astronauts.

Ancient people were often afraid of the sun, moon, and stars. This was because they thought these things were alive. The Egyptians believed that stars were the souls of dead people who had become gods. Others thought that since the stars looked smaller than the moon, they must be the moon's children.

But the Bible's first chapter (Genesis 1) points out that the sun, moon, and stars were created by God. This lets us know that they are not living beings to be feared.

Eclipses are a good example. An eclipse happens when the sun's light is blocked by the earth or moon for a short time. Usually, the moon is bright because it reflects the sun's light. But when the earth blocks that light, the moon looks like it's

disappearing. Also, when the moon comes between the earth and the sun, it looks to us like the sun is disappearing.

This was very frightening to people long ago. The Chaldeans, who lived close to the Israelites, thought that eclipses happened when the moon

Above: A complete solar eclipse.

Right: The sun's corona as seen during an eclipse.

was mad at the earth and turned its face away. The Chinese believed that an eclipse was caused by a dragon that ate the sun. That would be scary, wouldn't it?

But God told Jeremiah, "Don't be afraid of special signs in the sky, even though the other nations are afraid of them" (Jer. 10:12). God went on to reassure Jeremiah that the universe is under God's control (Jer. 10:12-13).

People who didn't know the Scriptures continued to be afraid of the skies for hundreds of years. Later, scientists learned that the heavenly bodies were not alive and that we should not fear them. Of course, that's what the Bible told us all along.

Until modern times, no one knew what the bottom of the ocean was like. People thought it was like the deserts, flat and sandy. They believed the ocean floor was mostly saucer shaped, and deepest in the middle.

But in the 1900s, oceanographers found that the sea has many deep valleys or canyons. The deepest of these canyons are called trenches. Some are amazingly deep.

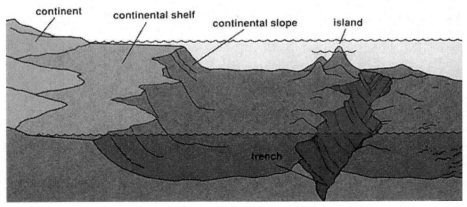

continent   continental shelf   continental slope   island

trench

For example, the Marianas trench in the Pacific is so deep that if you dropped Mt. Everest (29,000 feet high) into it, the peak would still be a mile below the surface.

Just as there are valleys in the ocean, so there are underwater mountains. In the Atlantic Ocean, there is a range of undersea mountains 10,000 miles long. A few of these rise above the surface and form islands.

But 3,000 years ago, the Bible mentioned both the valleys and the mountains of the sea. David wrote a psalm praising God for rescuing him from his enemies. He spoke of God being the maker of "the valleys of the sea" (2 Sam. 22:16 and Psalm 18:15, NIV). One of the questions God asks Job is, "Have you walked in the valleys of the sea?" (Job 38:16). The prophet Jonah talked about "mountains in the sea" (Jonah 2:6).

These parts of the Bible are not talking about oceanography. They are discussing man's relation to God. Even so, how did the writers of the Bible know about the mountains and valleys of the ocean thousands of years before scientists discovered them?

Somebody told them. And I have an idea who it was!

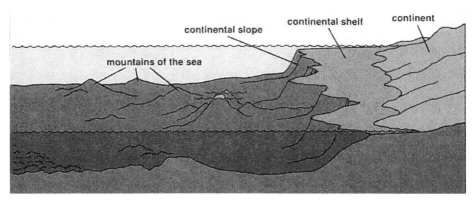

For thousands of years, doctors often treated sick people by a practice called "bleeding." They would cut a vein and drain blood from the patient. Why? Because people thought that diseases started in the blood. So, if you got rid of some blood, it would help you get well.

In December of 1799, George Washington became very ill. His doctors bled him four times in one day. In a few hours, he was dead.

In some parts of the world, folk healers still bleed their patients. But most doctors now know that bleeding doesn't help a sick person. It does just the opposite. That's because the blood carries to every part of our body the things we need to stay alive. Removing blood makes it harder for the blood that's left in the body to do its job.

And that's what the Bible said in Leviticus 17:11: "The life of the body is in the blood." Isn't it sad that, in George Washington's time, they didn't realize how true that verse is?

What the Bible tells us about blood is evidence that it is the Word of God, since no one else knew that at the time the Bible was written. But what the Bible doesn't say can also tell us that it came from God. And here's an example.

The Egyptians of Moses' time knew more about medicine than any other people. Yet they had some strange treatments. If a person had a deep splinter that got infected, they would put worm's blood or donkey manure on the sore spot. When children were sick, doctors often gave them skinned baby mice to eat. The list of such remedies is long.

Remember that Moses wrote Leviticus and most of the first five books of the Bible. He was raised as the King of Egypt's son. And "the Egyptians taught Moses everything they knew" (Acts 7:22). Yet not one of these weird treatments is mentioned in the Bible.

Other ancient books are filled with such harmful medical advice. How did Moses and the other writers of the Bible know to leave all of that out?

Lightning, thunder, and rainstorms have bothered man for thousands of years. In Bible times, people from Rome to Egypt to India thought lightning bolts were missiles thrown by the gods. The Chinese even thought lightning was a goddess. Her job was to flash light here and there to help the thunder god find the people he was mad at.

Since rain is so necessary to our life on earth, ancient people wondered what caused it. Some thought sprinkling water on the ground would help cause rain. Others tried to stab holes in the clouds with spears. Maybe the most unusual idea is found in one of the Vedas (holy books of the Hindu religion in India). It says to tie up a frog with its mouth propped open. If you tie him to the right tree and say the right words, rain will fall!

The Bible, too, talks about rain, lightning, and storms. But it includes none of the superstitious, fantastic ideas found in the other books written in those days. Instead of teaching that these forces of nature were living beings who often did crazy things, as many people believed, the Scriptures taught that the earth's weather follows rules and cycles. Notice Genesis 8:22:

> As long as the earth continues, planting and harvest, cold and hot, summer and winter, day and night will not stop.

Job 28:26 says God "made rules for the rain and set a path for a thunderstorm to follow." God told Jeremiah, "I have an agreement with day and night that they will always come at the right time" (Jeremiah 33:20).

Many years later, scientists would begin to discover the "rules for the rain" that Job talked about. We now have weathermen who know about the path of a thunderstorm.

Of course, all along the Bible had mentioned these laws of nature that we are still discovering. All along, Scripture reminds us that the laws of nature are really the laws of God.

Speaking of rain, exactly where does rain come from? Rainfall is part of a process called the water cycle. Here's how the cycle works: The sun evaporates water from the ocean. That water vapor rises and becomes clouds. This water in the clouds falls back to earth as rain, collects in streams and rivers, and makes its way back to the ocean. That process repeats itself again and again.

Scientists began to discover that water follows such a cycle about 300 years ago. Galileo came up with this idea in 1630. But amazingly, the Scriptures mentioned this centuries earlier.

rain

Amos 9:6 says that God "calls for the waters of the sea and pours them out on the land." Long before man discovered it, the Bible told us that the water from the sea ends up falling on the land.

Another verse talks about the water cycle in a little different way. Isaiah 55:10 shows that rain and snow return to the sky after watering the earth. "Rain and snow fall from the sky and they don't return without watering the ground."

How did Amos and Isaiah know where rain comes from? They weren't scientists. They were prophets who said they were just repeating God's message. And that must have been true, since God was the only one who knew about the water cycle 2,500 years ago.

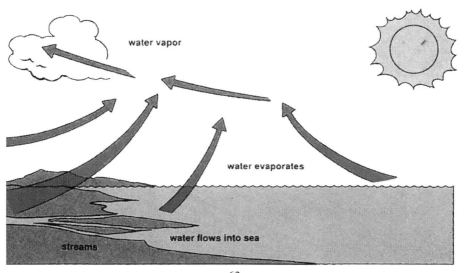

water vapor

water evaporates

water flows into sea

streams

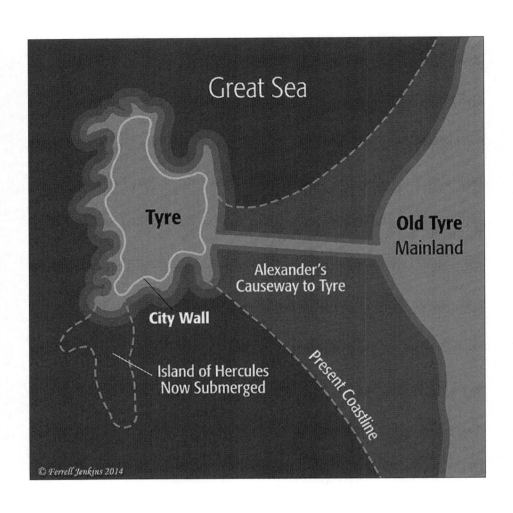

Fulfilled Prophecy

Sometimes, God gives a message to a person for that person to share with others. The person God gives such a message to is called a prophet. His message is called a prophecy.

Usually, a prophecy is mainly for the people of that time and place. But sometimes God enables a prophet to predict the future!

Long before Jesus was born, many prophets predicted the future by telling about him. For example, more than 700 years before Christ, the prophet Micah wrote,

> But you, Bethlehem Ephrathah, are one of the smallest towns in Judah. But from you will come one who will rule Israel for me. Micah 5:2

Many years later, some wise men came to Jerusalem looking for the baby Jesus. Herod asked the teachers of the Law where Christ would be born. "They answered, 'In the town of Bethlehem in Judah. The prophet wrote about this in the Scriptures" (Matthew 2:5). So those who were familiar with the Scriptures knew that Jesus would be born in Bethlehem. They just didn't know when.

But when the wise men saw his star, they knew the time had come. So they went to Bethlehem as the Scripture had said, and of course, he was there.

Modern Bethlehem, with the Church of the Nativity at top center.

Another prophecy that came true is the one made by David in Psalm 16:10. David lived about 1,000 years before Christ. He wrote,

> You will not leave me in the grave. You will not let your Holy One rot.

But David wasn't talking about himself. As Peter said in Acts 2:31, "David was talking about the Christ rising from death." Peter was a witness to Jesus rising from death. But David had predicted it 1,000 years before.

Wouldn't it be amazing if someone could tell fifteen facts about a person—and do it 800 years before the person was born? Well, that's what the Old Testament prophet Isaiah did. His description of Jesus was so detailed it could have fit no one else. Notice how well Jesus fits all fifteen of Isaiah's predictions in the chart below.

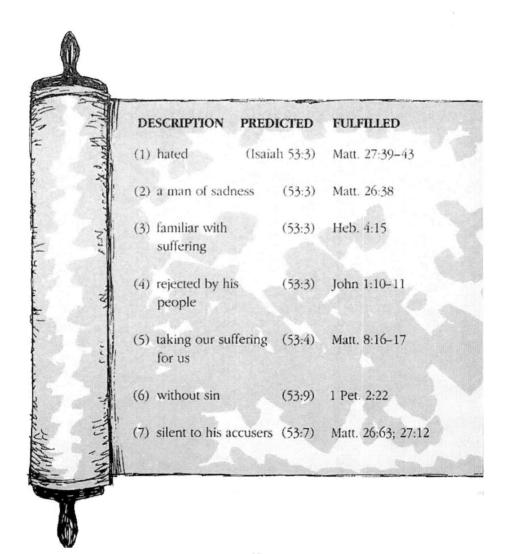

DESCRIPTION	PREDICTED	FULFILLED
(1) hated	(Isaiah 53:3)	Matt. 27:39–43
(2) a man of sadness	(53:3)	Matt. 26:38
(3) familiar with suffering	(53:3)	Heb. 4:15
(4) rejected by his people	(53:3)	John 1:10–11
(5) taking our suffering for us	(53:4)	Matt. 8:16–17
(6) without sin	(53:9)	1 Pet. 2:22
(7) silent to his accusers	(53:7)	Matt. 26:63; 27:12

Early Christians used Isaiah's prophecy as a starting place to tell people who Jesus was and what he did. For example, in Acts chapter 8 a man from the African country of Ethiopia was reading Isaiah 53. He was curious about who Isaiah was describing. When the man asked Philip that question, Philip "started with this same Scripture and told the man the Good News about Jesus" (Acts 8:35). And that Scripture about Jesus was written 800 years before his birth.

DESCRIPTION	PREDICTED	FULFILLED
(8) taking our sins on himself	(53:5)	1 Cor. 15:3
(9) taking our punishment	(53:5)	1 Pet. 2:24–25
(10) treated like a criminal	(53:12)	Luke 22:37
(11) asking for our forgiveness	(53:12)	Luke 23:34
(12) treated unjustly	(53:8)	Matt. 27:24
(13) buried with rich people	(53:9)	Matt. 27:57–60
(14) raised from death	(53:10)	Luke 24:6–8
(15) honored	(53:12)	Phil. 2:9–11

Tyre was a powerful and wealthy city. Part of the city was on the coast, but some of the people lived on an island a half mile out in the ocean. The people of Tyre were famous for making purple dye and beautiful glassware. But they were also very evil.

About 586 B.C., the prophet Ezekiel reported what God had told him about Tyre. First, he said, Tyre would be attacked by Nebuchadnezzar's Babylonian army and later by other nations. Next, the city would be destroyed so completely that its wood and rock would be scraped up and thrown into the sea. It would not be rebuilt; it would be just a place for fishermen to spread their nets.

Shortly after this prophecy, Nebuchadnezzar did surround and attack the mainland part of the city. The battle went on for thirteen years. Finally, the Babylonians broke down the walls and tore up the city. But many of the people of Tyre escaped in boats to the island. So Nebuchadnezzar, even though he conquered the city, didn't fulfill Ezekiel's prophecy.

But 250 years later, Alexander the Great and his Greek army wanted to capture the island city. How could a marching

army get to it? There was a half-mile of water between them and the island. Then someone had an idea: Why not take the ruins of the mainland city and dump them in the ocean? This would make a walkway out to the island. So they scraped up all the wood, rock, and dust from the old city and built a road for the army to attack on. It worked perfectly, and the job of destroying Tyre was completed.

Later, another city called Tyre was built nearby, but not on the same location. For 2,000 years, fishermen have used the spot where old Tyre was as a place to spread their nets.

It all happened just as the prophet had said in Ezekiel 26:1-14. But how could

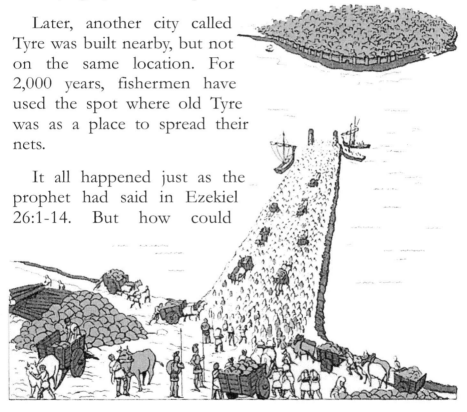

Ezekiel have known what would happen 250 years in the future? There's only one explanation. It was just as Ezekiel said: "The Lord spoke his word to me." (26:1)

The ruins of Babylon in modern-day Iraq.

Babylon was the capital of the Chaldean empire and the mightiest city in the world. Its walls were 200 feet high and 187 feet thick. The huge brass gates and 300-foot-high towers for watchmen made it seem impossible to defeat. But while Babylon was at the height of its power, God's prophets said it would end.

Isaiah wrote, "Babylon is the most beautiful of all kingdoms. The Babylonians are very proud of it. But God will destroy it like Sodom and Gomorrah." (Isa. 13:19) Sodom and Gomorrah were two wicked cities that had been wiped out and never rebuilt.

Another prophet, Jeremiah, said this:

> This is what the Lord all-powerful says; "Babylon's thick wall will be completely pulled down and her high gates burned ... No people or animals will live in it. It will be an empty ruin forever." (Jer. 51:58, 62)

Long after Isaiah and Jeremiah were dead, the Persians captured Babylon. Later, Alexander the Great and his Greek army took it from the Persians.

Alexander was one of the greatest military men in history. He ruled a huge area from Greece to India. He decided to rebuild Babylon and make it his capital city. But after giving the order to rebuild it, Alexander got sick and died at the age of 33. His order was not carried out. Even the most powerful man in the world cannot do something if God says it will not happen!

Six hundred years later, a Roman ruler named Julian (who didn't believe the Bible) was leading an army to fight the Persians. Part of Babylon's walls were still standing. To keep the Persians from using those walls, he had what was left of them completely leveled. And so a man who tried to keep people from believing the Bible actually helped make its words come true.

In its days of glory, Babylon had the most beautiful gardens in the world. Those Hanging Gardens were considered one of the seven wonders of the ancient world. But today the spot where Babylon stood is a barren desert. Just as the Bible said it would be.

The Edomites were a powerful nation for hundreds of years. They were neighbors of the Israelites. In a way, they were also relatives, because the people of Edom were the descendants of Esau. The Israelites were the descendants of Esau's brother, Jacob. But the two groups were not usually on friendly terms with each other. Because the Edomites mistreated Israel and even stole from God's temple, God decided to punish them.

Several prophets told what would happen to them. Obadiah gave this message from God:

> Your home is up high, you say to yourself, "No one can bring me down to the ground" … "I will bring you down from there," says the Lord. (Obadiah 3, 4)

The Edomites lived in forts built high in the rocks. They were sure no one could ever defeat them. But Isaiah said their strong cities would become deserted:

The ruins of Petra, one of the fortresses of the Nabateans.

God will make it an empty wasteland; it will have nothing left in it ... Thorns will take over the strong towers, and wild bushes will grow in the walled cities. I will be a home for wild dogs and a place for owls to live. (Isaiah 34:11, 13)

Jeremiah had a similar message:

"Edom will be destroyed like the cities of Sodom and Gomorrah and the towns around them," says the Lord. "No one will live there! No one will stay in Edom". (Jeremiah 49:18)

And that is just what happened. Within the next 200 years, the Edomites were defeated by the Arabs and later by the Nabateans. Petra, the capital city of the Nabateans, contained many temples carved into solid rock. It can still be visited today. But no one lives there. Some ruins of Edomite cities have also been found. But there, too, the only living things are weeds and wild animals. And even they help show us that the Bible is true.

There were several groups of people who were strong and doing well when the Bible said they were going to be punished for their sins. The Moabites and the Ammonites are good examples. Several prophets predicted the end of those nations. Ezekiel, for instance, reported that God said:

> I will give Moab, along with the Ammonites, to the people of the East as their possession. Then, along with the Ammonites, Moab will not be a nation anymore ... And they will know that I am the Lord. (Ezekiel 25:10-11)

The Moabite stone, erected by Mesha, king of Moab, and dating back to about 850 B.C. It contains over thirty lines of writing in ancient Moabite.

The Moabites and the Ammonites were defeated by the Babylonians and the Persians. (Both came from the east.) By the year 70 A.D., both Moabites and Ammonites had disappeared—just as the Scripture had said hundreds of years earlier.

Nineveh (like Babylon) was a powerful city surrounded by huge walls. But God's prophet, Nahum, said that the city would fall and a flood would help its enemies capture it (Nahum 1:8, 2:6). Zephaniah (2:13-14). He added that it would be deserted and become just a place to keep flocks and herds.

Nineveh was captured by its enemies in 612 B.C. when the Tigris River flooded and burst part of the walls, letting the attacking army in. About 200 years later, the Greek army

Two Elamite warriors carrying bows and a quiver, a limestone relief from Nineveh, about 668-633 B.C.

passed through the area. They reported that there was only a pile of rubble where the mighty city had been.

As you might guess, it is still deserted today. But that place is good for one thing: grazing flocks of sheep. In fact, its modern name means "Mound of Many Sheep."

These are just a few of the many predictions of the Bible

coming true exactly as the Scripture had said. But this should not surprise us. Jesus himself told the apostle John, "Write the things you see, what is now and what will happen later" (Revelation 1:19).

But why are all these predictions in the Bible? One reason is that they help us have confidence in the Scripture and in the God who gave it. I like what D. James Kennedy wrote in his book *Why I Believe* (p. 26):

> Predictions are also promises. I believe that God gave us over two thousand predictions in order that we may learn to believe his promises. God promised that the walls of Jerusalem would be rebuilt; that the walls of Babylon would never be rebuilt; that the walls of Tyre would be destroyed; that Sidon would continue—so that we may believe his promises.

Evidence from Archaeology

The Old Testament mentions a group of people called the Hittites many times. Some of them lived to the north of the Israelites. Others lived with the Israelites in the land of Canaan. Genesis 23:10 explains Abraham bought some land from Ephron the Hittite. Later Esau married a Hittite woman. Two of David's fighting men, Uriah and Ahimelech, were Hittites.

But until about one hundred years ago, no one had found any trace or mention of the Hittites anywhere—except in the Bible. People who didn't believe the Bible said, "There's no evidence that there ever was such a people as the Hittites. If they really existed, someone else would have written about them. Or archaeologists would have found remains of their work. This shows that the Bible is wrong."

But Bible believers said, "That doesn't mean the Bible is wrong. Maybe we just haven't found the evidence of the Hittites yet. If the Scripture says it, it must be true. Just wait."

Sure enough—in 1906 a German named Hugo Winckler was digging in the land we now call Turkey. He found the city that was the Hittite capital. He also found many clay tablets written in the Hittite language. Of course, it took many years before anyone could figure out how to read it. But eventually they did. One interesting thing about Hittite writing was that sometimes the Hittites wrote from right to left on one line and then from left to right on the next.

Further proof that the Hittites had existed was found on clay tablets in Egypt. These clay tablets told of a great battle between Ramses II of Egypt and the Hittites in 1287 B.C. Ramses was even captured by them for a while. He was later rescued when the Egyptians finally won. Archaeologists have even discovered pictures of Hittites drawn by Egyptian artists.

These archaeological discoveries showed that the Bible was correct and that the doubters were completely wrong.

General view of the ruins of the Hittite capital, Hattusa, located about 100 miles east of Ankara in Turkey.

One of the most interesting stories in the Bible is the one in Daniel chapter 5. It tells about Belshazzar, the last king of Babylon. Belshazzar threw a giant party for a thousand guests. He served them their drinks in cups stolen from God's Temple in Jerusalem.

Suddenly, a hand appeared, wrote four words on the wall, and then disappeared. The frightened king tried to find out what the words meant. Finally Daniel was called in. Because God revealed to Daniel the meaning of each word, he was able to interpret those words for the king. You can read about the meanings of those words in Daniel 5:26, but what they meant to Belshazzar was that Belshazzar's time as king was

Sixth-century Babylonian tablet describing a number of historical events, including the taking of Jerusalem.

over. He was killed that night, and the Medes and Persians took over Babylon.

For many years, unbelievers said that the story couldn't be true, because Belshazzar was not the last king of Babylon. According to the ancient historical writings, Nabonidus was the last king—and there never was a king named Belshazzar.

But in the 1900's, archaeologists digging in the old city of Ur found many tablets that the Babylonians had written on. Some of them were from the time of Nabonidus. And guess what they said? King Nabonidus left the country for several years. While he was gone, he left his son to rule as king. That son was named Belshazzar. He was killed the day the Medes and Persians took over Babylon.

And that, of course, was exactly what the book of Daniel had said.

In school, William Ramsay was an excellent student. Growing up in Scotland, he won several awards for his good grades. And he was especially interested in things that happened long ago. He wanted to learn things about the past that no one else had ever discovered. He made up his mind to learn about the ancient Greeks by actually going to the ruins of their cities. He didn't want to just read about it— he wanted to dig and search until he became an expert on what life was like 2,000 years ago.

But William Ramsay didn't believe the Bible. For example, he didn't believe that the book of Acts in the New Testament was written by Luke, as many Christians believe. He said it was written one hundred years after the time of Luke by someone who didn't know what he was writing about. Ramsay thought the writer just made up some of the stories because they would sound good.

In 1880, Ramsay went on his first expedition to the places described in the book of Acts. He spent many years traveling, digging, and studying ancient writings in that part of the world. He was sure he could prove that the book of Acts was full of mistakes and could not be believed.

And what did he discover? For one thing, he was the first to find out that the city of Iconium was not part of the district of Lycaonia, as the experts in his day used to think. He

This Greek inscription on a Roman arch in Thessalonica helped convince Ramsay that the book of Acts was accurate

also found that the people of Lycaonia even spoke their own language. But the book of Acts, which Ramsay didn't believe, had already explained that fact, in chapter 14 verses 1-11.

Ramsay had not expected his discoveries to prove that the book of Acts was right. But, in fact, the more he discovered, the more he found that Acts was not full of mistakes, after all. He was most impressed with how the writer got those small, seemingly unimportant details exactly right. That, he claimed, was the mark of a writer who knows what he is talking about and is careful to tell everything correctly.

William Ramsay went on to become one of the world's greatest experts on life in New Testament days. His research led him to write many excellent books that show how accurate and believable the New Testament is. In one of those books, he announced that he had become a Christian.

The story of William Ramsay is one more reason we can have confidence that the Bible is true.

Another biblical story that unbelievers used to doubt is found in Genesis 14. There, four kings had come all the way from Babylonia to fight five kings in Abraham's area near the Dead Sea. Abraham's nephew, Lot, was captured by the four invaders. Abraham then got a small army together and rescued Lot.

"That couldn't have happened," the doubters said. "It was all made up. The Babylonians didn't have any dealings with the people in Palestine in those days. And anyway, people didn't travel that far back then—especially not to fight."

But in the past hundred years, archaeologists have dug up much information about Babylonia in Abraham's time. It turns out that Babylonia did have dealings with Palestine. They even controlled part of it. And the people from Abraham's area fought to get out from under Babylonian rule more than once. The story in Genesis 14 is obviously one of those times.

Egyptian tomb painting from Thebes

Another story that doubters used to criticize is found in Genesis 40—part of the story of Joseph in Egypt. Some people argued that the part about the butler picking grapes to make wine for the king of Egypt wasn't true because there is no evidence that grapes ever grew in Egypt.

But eventually, that evidence was found. In the Egyptian city of Thebes, a painting on a tomb shows Egyptians picking grapes and making wine.

In ancient times, people often carved their writing on stones or clay tablets. This is lucky for us, because those tablets can last for thousands of years. Kings, especially, liked to order tablets carved that would tell of their accomplishments. It is always interesting when these carvings tell of people or events that are also mentioned in the Bible.

For example, Shalmaneser III (king of Assyria from 859-824 B.C.) tells about his dealings with two kings of Israel, Ahab and Jehu. He even has a drawing of Jehu. Another king of Assyria, Sennacherib, tells the story of his attack on Jerusalem when Hezekiah was king there. That story is also told in the Bible (2 Kings 18:13-19:37).

Right: The Taylor Prism, a hexagonal cylinder, recounts Senacharib's raid into Judah about 701 B.B.
Above: The "Black Obelisk of Shalmaneser" shows Jehu bowing before Shalmaneser III.

But Sennacherib leaves out one important part: why his army wasn't able to capture Jerusalem. That isn't surprising, since those kings didn't usually tell about their losses, only their victories.

That's another way the Bible is different from other ancient books. It tells everything that needs to be told—victories and defeats, the good and the bad.

The value of these and many other discoveries is that they help to show over and over again that the people, places, and events described in the Bible were real people, places, and events.

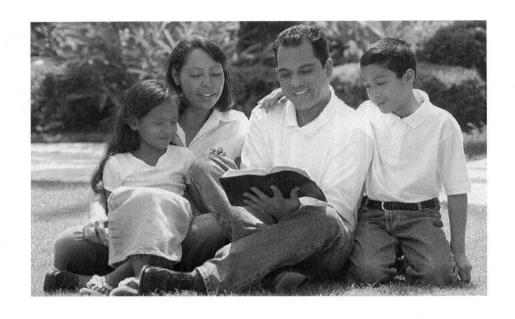

More Good Reasons

In many ways, the Bible is the most amazing book ever written. It's really a collection of books. The earliest was written about 1,500 years before Christ. The last book (Revelation) was finished almost 100 years after Jesus' birth. That means it took about 1,600 years to complete the Bible.

Papyrus fragments of John 18:31-33, the earliest copy of any New Testament book, dated about A.D. 150. Found in Egypt.

At least forty different people did part of the writing. And they were all very different! There was Luke (a doctor), Peter (a fisherman), Joshua (an army leader), Amos (a sheep herder), Matthew (a tax collector), Solomon (a king), Nehemiah (a king's servant), and many others we know nothing about.

They wrote from many different places. Moses was traveling in the wilderness. Paul was in prison during part of the time he wrote. Daniel lived in a palace. John was on a lonely island. David was fighting enemies or being chased by them when writing some of the Psalms.

The Bible was first written in three languages. The New Testament was in Greek. Most of the Old Testament was written in Hebrew, but part of Daniel was in Aramaic. The

Bible is also made up of many kinds of writings. Part of it is the history of a group of people. Some books follow one person's life. Part of it is poetry; some of the books are collections of laws. There are letters to people and books that tell the future.

Yet this book, written by so many people, over such a long period of time, in different languages, and different places, still all fits together to tell one story of how we got here and where we're going. Things that began in the first book are finished in the last one. Genesis (2:9) tells where God first put the tree of life. Revelation (22:1-3) tells where it is now. Genesis tells the cause of the first sadness. Revelation tells when tears will end.

No man would ever have been able to put together a collection like this!

For thousands of years, unbelievers have tried to destroy the Bible, but they have all failed.

This began while the Bible was still being written. In ancient Israel, an evil king, Jehoiakim, burned the book of Jeremiah because it told what he had done wrong. But God helped Jeremiah to write it all again—plus even more (Jeremiah 36).

The Romans and the leaders of the Jews tried to stop Paul by putting him in prison. The prison he was in disappeared long ago. But the letters he wrote while he was there are still helping people today.

In the year 303, the Roman emperor, Diocletian, ordered all copies of the books of the Bible destroyed. He thought

that he had succeeded. He even had a medal engraved that said, "The Christian religion is destroyed." But it was Diocletian who died, not the Bible.

Voltaire was a Frenchman who lived in the 1700s. He was a famous writer, but he didn't believe the Scriptures. In fact, he made fun of the Bible. Voltaire predicted that within a hundred years, the Bible would be gone. But fifty years after his death, the printing press he had owned was being used to print Bibles. And the house he had lived in was made into a center for distributing them.

No matter how hard evil men have tried to get rid of the Bible, they haven't been able to. And today, those men are dead. But the Bible remains.

There has never been a book like the Bible. More books have been written about it than any other. The message in the Bible has given artists and musicians their ideas for many of the world's greatest masterpieces.

But most important of all, the Scriptures continue to change people's lives. No one can count the number of people who have turned from a life of crime, or quit mistreating others, or stopped using drugs or alcohol after being touched by the Bible's story.

One of those people was John Newton, who lived in the late 1700s. John did many evil things—in fact, he spent about ten years buying and selling people as slaves. But during one frightening storm on the high seas, his ship nearly sank, and afterward John started reading the Bible. It changed his life. Reading Jesus' story in Luke 15 about the runaway son, John realized that God loves even those of us who have done much wrong, and he is eager for us to turn to him.

John Newton became a well-known preacher who worked to end the slave business in England. He also wrote several hymns we still sing today—including "Amazing Grace."

Charles Colson had an important White House job working for President Nixon. But he broke the law and was sent to prison. There, he began reading the Bible and turned his life over to Jesus Christ. Then, besides writing best-selling books about the Christian faith, he spent the rest of his life going to prisons everywhere telling people about Christ.

Here's another example: Billy Sunday was an alcoholic pro baseball player who was saved and became one of the most famous preachers of his day. Or another: C. S. Lewis was an atheist as a young man but became a believer and went on to author many Christian classics, including the *Chronicles of Narnia.*

Many books are interesting and helpful to read. But only the Bible tells us everything we need to know about the things that are most important. As 2 Peter 1:3 says, "Jesus has the power of God. His power has given us everything we need to live and to serve God."

Throughout this book, I have tried to tell some of the many reasons we believe the Bible. Each of these reasons is one more bit of evidence that the Bible came from God.

But what does the Bible itself say? Over and over again, the writers wrote things like this: "This is what the Lord says ... " (Jeremiah 31:2, NIV) or "The Lord spoke his word to me ... "(Ezekiel 24:1).

The Bible tells us that God used the Holy Spirit to tell men what to write. Paul said, "God has shown us these things through the Spirit" (1 Corinthians 2:10). He said the same thing about the Old Testament: "The Holy Spirit spoke the truth to your ancestors through Isaiah the prophet" (Acts 28:25).

The word we use to say the Bible came from God is "inspiration" or "inspired." That means that God let the writers know what they should write. We don't know exactly how this took place, but Paul wrote in 2 Timothy 3:16 (NIV), "All Scripture is God-breathed." Isn't that an interesting way to describe it? However God gave his message to the writers, it was like he was breathing on them. To help us understand better, Peter adds this explanation:

> Most of all you must understand this: No prophecy in the Scriptures ever comes from the prophet's own interpretation. No prophecy ever came from what a person wanted to say. But men led by the Holy Spirit spoke words from God. (2 Peter 1:20—21)

The Bible writers wanted to be sure that we understood that they were not just giving their own ideas. Rather, God himself was giving them information to pass on to us.

Because of that, we can be sure that the Bible is God's message to us. As we read it carefully, let's remember 2 Timothy 3:15: "Since you were a child you have known the holy Scriptures which are able to make you wise. And that wisdom leads to salvation through faith in Christ Jesus."

End Notes

Part 1: Clues from Man

[1] C. S. Lewis, *Mere Christianity* (New York: McMillan, 1952), 5.

[2] Lewis, *Mere Christianity*, 106.

[3] A. J. Hoover, *The Case for Christian Theism* (Grand Rapids: Baker Book House, 1976), 89-91.

Part 2: Clues from Nature

[1] Alan Hayward, *God Is* (Nashville: Thomas Nelson, 1978) 119.

[2] Don England, *God, Are You Really There?* (Nashville: 20th-Century Christian, 1989) 31.

[3] Lawrence Richards, *It Couldn't Just Happen* (Dallas: Word Publishing, 1989) 104-105.

Part 3: Clues from the Human Body

[1] Paul Brand and Philip Yancey, *In His Image* (Grand Rapids: Zondervan, 1984) 55.

[2] England, *God, Are You Really There?* 38.

[3] Francis S. Collins, *The Language of God*. (New York: Free Press, 2006), p. 2, 3.

Part 4: Clues about God from the Universe

[1] Hugh Ross, *The Improbable Planet* (Chicago, Baker Book House. 2016) 35.

[2] Hugh Ross, *The Creator and the Cosmos* (Colorado Springs: Navpress, 1993) 105-114, 123-132. and Hayward, *God Is*, 61-68.

[3] Quoted in D. James Kennedy and Jerry Newcombe, *What If Jesus Had Never Been Born?* (Dallas: Word Publishing, 1994) 100.

End Notes

[4]Kennedy, *What If,* 99.

[5] Eric Barrett and David Fisher, eds. *Scientists Who Believe* (Chicago: Moody Press, 1984), 5-6.

[6] Barrett and Fisher, *Scientists Who Believe*, 110.

[7]Ross, *The Creator of the Cosmos*, 114.

[8] Ross, *The Creator and the Cosmos*, 114-115.

[9] Hayward, *God Is*, 55-56.

Part 5: Faith in God Changes People and the World

[1]Clark Pinnock, *A Case for Faith*, (Minneapolis: Bethany House, 1980) 99-100.

Part 6: The Bible Reveals the True God

[1]John Piper, *The Pleasures of God*, (Portland: Multnomah Press, 1991) 91.

Bibliography

Kenny Barfield. *Why the Bible is Number One*. Grand Rapids, Michigan: Baker Book House, 1988.

Eric Barrett and David Fisher, eds. *Scientists Who Believe*. Chicago: Moody Press, 1984.

Batsell Barrett Baxter. *I Believe Because*. Grand Rapids: Baker Book House, 1971.

Paul Brand and Philip Yancey. *In His Image*. Grand Rapids: Zondervan, 1984.

F. F. Bruce. *The New Testament Documents-Are They Reliable?* Grand Rapids: Eerdman's Publishing, 1959..

Francis S. Collins. *The Language of God*. New York: Free Press, 2006.

Don England. *God, Are You Really There?* Nashville: 20th Century Christian, 1989.

Don Hayward. *God Is*. Nashville: Thomas Nelson, 1976.

A.J. Hoover. *The Case for Christian Theism*. Grand Rapids: Baker Book House, 1976.

D. James Kennedy. *Why I Believe*. Dallas: Word Publishing, 1981.

D. James Kennedy and Jerry Newcombe. *What If Jesus Had Never Been Born?* Dallas: Word Publishing, 1994.

C.S. Lewis. *Mere Christianity*. New York: Macmillan, 1952.

Josh McDowell. *Evidence That Demands a Verdict*. San Bernadino: Here's Life Publishers, 1979.

S. I. McMillen. *None of These Diseases*. Old Tappan, New Jersey: Fleming H Revell, 1984.

Clark Pinnock.. *A Case for Faith*. Minneapolis: Bethany House,

Bibliography

1980.

John Piper. *The Pleasures of God*. Portland: Multnomah Press, 1991.

William Ramsay. *St. Paul the Traveler and Roman Citizen*. Grand Rapids: Baker Book House, 1982.

Lawrence Richards. *It Couldn't Just Happen*. Dallas: Word Publishing, 1989.

Hugh Ross. *The Creator and the Cosmos*. Colorado Springs: Navpress, 1993.

Hugh Ross, *The Improbable Planet.* Chicago, Baker Book House. 2016).

J. A. Thompson. *The Bible and Archaeology*. Grand Rapids: Eerdmans Publishing, 1972

Made in the USA
Columbia, SC
23 March 2020

89518901R00059